GW01606506

Published 1978 by The Hamlyn Publishing Group Limited
London · New York · Sydney · Toronto Astronaut House, Feltham, Middlesex, England.
© Copyright 1978 by the Hamlyn Publishing Group Limited

All rights reserved. No part of this publication may be reproduced, stored in a retrieval system, or transmitted, in any form or by any means, electronic, mechanical, photocopying, recording or otherwise, without the permission of The Hamlyn Publishing Group Limited

ISBN 0 600 34537 8 Printed in Great Britain
Some of the stories in this book have appeared in storybooks previously published by the Hamlyn Publishing Group Limited

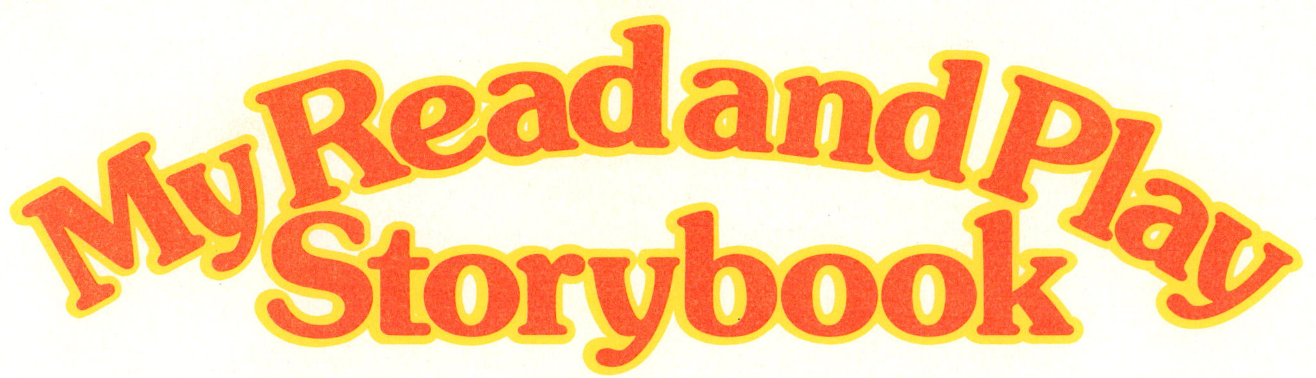

My Read and Play Storybook

Stories, puzzles and rhymes

edited by Jenny Dennis

illustrations by
Caroline Sharpe, Gwen Green and David Barnett

Hamlyn
London · New York · Sydney · Toronto

Contents

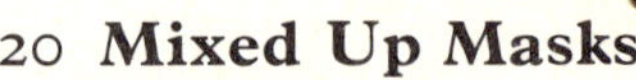

The Univited Guest

It was New Year's Eve and the woodcutter's family, who lived alone in the forest, decided to have a party.

'But there is so little to eat,' said Truda, eldest of the children.

Outside it was snowing, but inside the cottage all was cosy. 'Perhaps the New Year will bring us good fortune,' Truda was saying when Jonathan, her brother, interrupted.

'Listen, was that a knock at the door?' Truda and Jonathan slowly pulled back the heavy oak door, and there before them stood a traveller wrapped in a big cloak.

'May I come in and take shelter?' he asked in a gentle voice.

'Most certainly,' said Truda. 'You are welcome to stay with us this cold night.'

As the stranger moved across to the fire, Truda poured him out some hot potato soup. 'You must join in our New Year's party,' said the woodcutter.

'You are most kind. Thank you,' said their visitor. So the woodcutter, his wife and six children, all sat down together at the table, and the visitor smiled.

'You have so little, yet you are willing to share it with me,' he said. 'Maybe you will be surprised when you see who I am!'

At the same moment he flung back his cloak and on his head was a golden crown studded with jewels.

'It is the king!' gasped Jonathan.

'Yes, I am your king. I wanted to find who were the kindest of my people,' he said. He crossed to the door and opened it for the woodcutter and his children. Standing outside was a fine coach – indeed it was the royal coach. 'Now we shall go to the palace,' said the king.

The children were so surprised and thrilled that before they knew it they were all seated at a very different table in the dining hall at the palace.

'This is a real party,' said Stephen, the youngest of the children.

'The first of many parties we shall enjoy together, I hope,' said the king.

The Wisdom of Wung Loo

One day a young Chinese boy, named Chee Foo, was fishing on the river bank. When he pulled in his net he found to his amazement that instead of catching a fish he had landed an old black money purse. When he opened the purse he gasped, for it was full of golden coins.

'This is a fortune,' said Chee Foo, 'I must take it to the magistrate.'

Wung Loo was a clever and wise old magistrate. 'Already Li Chang, the sandal maker, has inquired about the purse he lost whilst walking by the riverside,' he said. 'He has offered ten golden coins as a reward. I will send for him.'

Li Chang soon arrived, a rather sly and crafty looking man. In front of the magistrate and Chee Foo he emptied the purse and counted the coins.

'There are ten missing,' he said. 'Just the amount of the reward.'

Wung Loo nodded and smiled.

'Have you taken any out?' he asked Chee Foo.

'Oh, no, your excellency!'

Wung Loo took up the purse.

'If your lost purse contained ten more coins than this one, worthy Li Chang, then this purse cannot be the one you lost. I therefore hand it back to Chee Foo!'

Three Skiers

Here are three pictures of skiers enjoying themselves in the mountains. They look exactly alike, but the artist has played a game with you. Look carefully for the odd picture out and see how many deliberate mistakes you can find in it.

Japanese Maze

Hanako, the Japanese girl, has made tea, but Taro has no idea how to find his way through the maze to reach her. Can you decide which way he should go?

Odd One Out

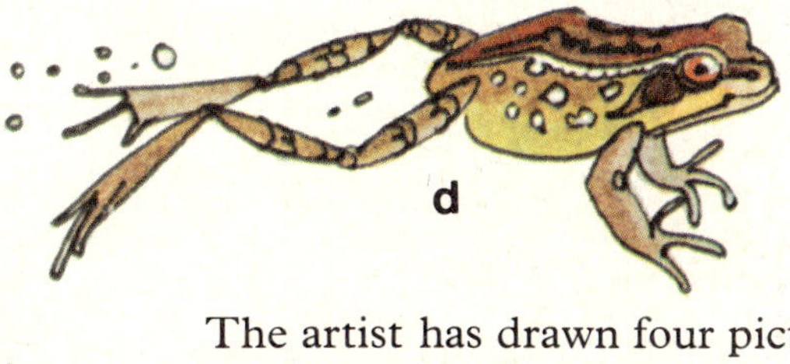

The artist has drawn four pictures – a butterfly, a frog, a parrot and a wasp. Which of these is the odd one out?

The Christmas Goose

This is the tale of Martin, the old gardener and his wife, Maria. They were good people, but poor, and they could never afford meat for their table. For their meals they had only the vegetables that Martin grew.

Christmas was coming and they longed for a roast goose for the festive season.

'I have an idea,' said Martin. 'Let us buy a baby goose now, and if we feed it well, it will be plump and tasty by the time Christmas is here.'

So they bought a cheap gosling. She was beautiful with fine feathers and sad eyes. They called her Joanna and built her a shed to live in. In the cold weather the two old people kept Joanna in their warm house and soon she was waddling about freely.

Martin and Maria, who had no-one except each other, spoiled the goose, who was now becoming very fat. They talked to her and petted her and she grew completely tame.

Christmas was almost upon them. In all the houses hams were being prepared and the geese were plucked. 'It is time for you to get Joanna ready now,' Martin said one day.

'What!' exclaimed Maria. 'I am not going to kill our dear little friend. You must do it.' But her husband had no intention of killing their pet goose.

It was clear that neither of them was willing to kill the goose. They thought about it for a long time and at last reached a decision. They would take Joanna to the butcher instead, but she gave them such a sad look that they did not have the heart to touch her.

And so there were three for Christmas dinner – Martin and Maria and the plump, happy Joanna. And instead of roast goose, they ate sprouts, carrots and chicory salad. But it did not matter. Their little friend meant more to them than the tastiest feast in the world.

FAIRGROUND TARGET

Hit Aunt Sally

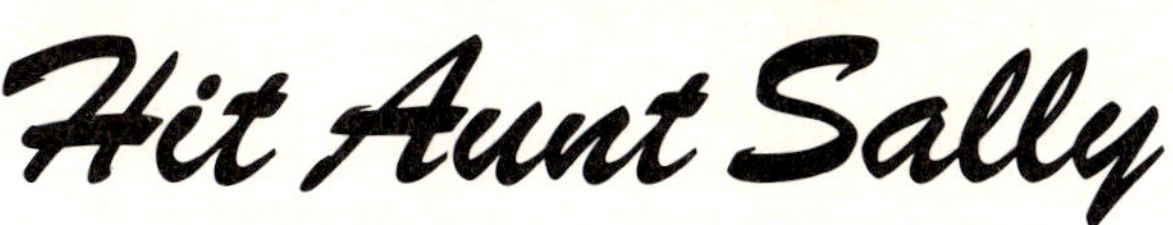

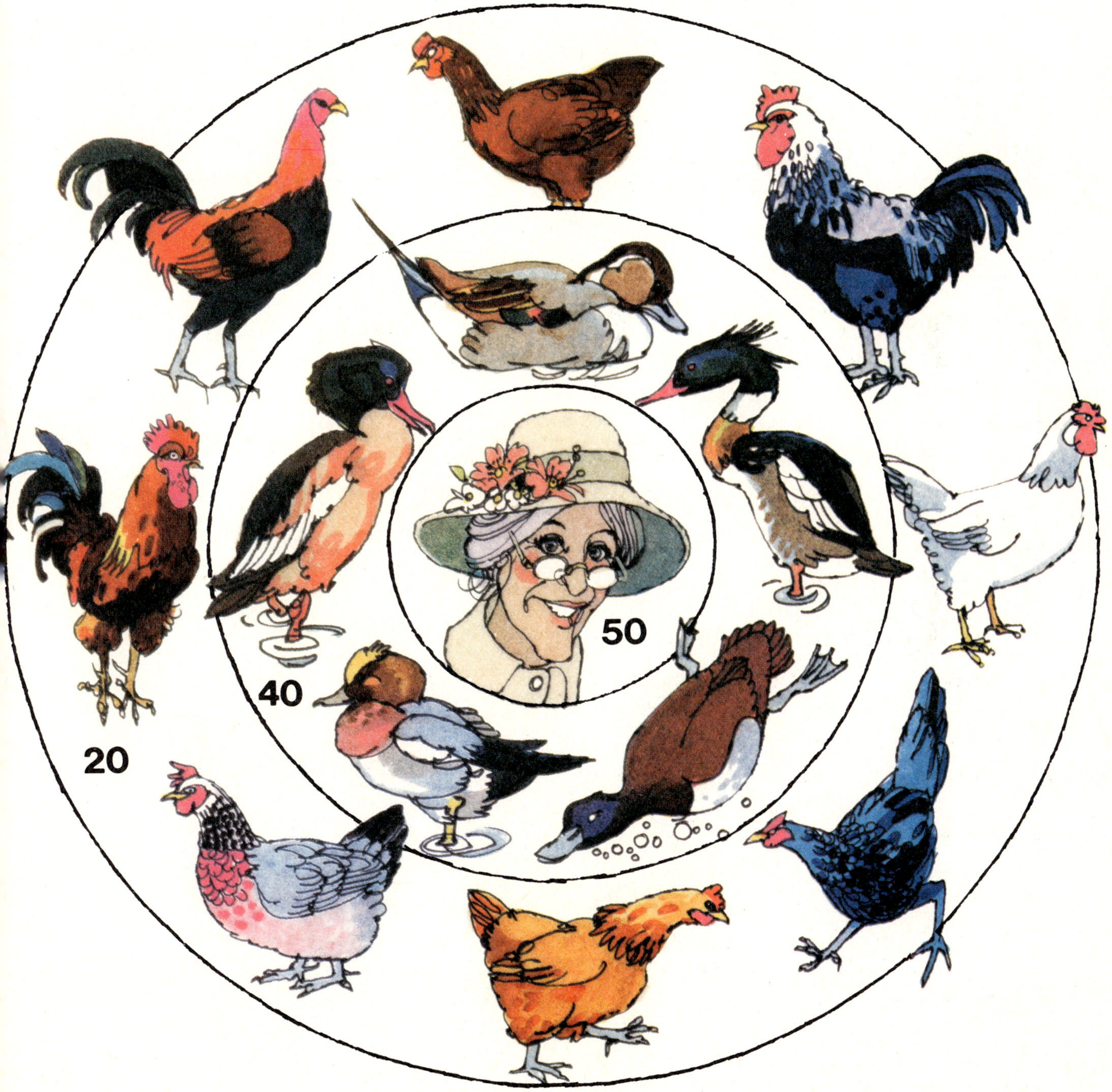

You will need two coloured counters for each player. Take it in turns to play, using the counters as you would in tiddly winks. The aim is to flick the counters onto the board and see how many times you can hit Aunt Sally.

A direct hit on the target scores 50, the ducks score 40, and the chickens only give 20 points. The highest score you could total in six throws is 300. Off you go and see who wins!

The Mermaid

Once upon a sunny summer's day
When I went down to the beach to play,
I think it was at three o'clock,
I saw a mermaid on a rock.
And she was gazing out to sea
But turned around when she heard me,
And, combing out her golden hair,
Said, 'Don't you know it's rude to stare?'
I didn't know what I should say,
I don't meet mermaids every day,
She mocked me with her green, green eyes,
And laughed aloud at my surprise.
I thought that underneath the seas
She really must be quite a tease,
But then a wave came rolling on,
Covered the rock, and she was gone.

Sparrows' Supper

Five little sparrows,
Twenty grains of wheat.
How many grains
Does each sparrow eat?

The Old Wooden Pencil Box

The old wooden pencil box was very upset. Robert didn't want to use it any more. All through the holidays it had been pushed away at the back of the toy cupboard – and it had been so looking forward to going back to school.

Besides, it had been to school for years. It had been to school with Robert since he was five – and with Robert's daddy, when he had been a little boy – and before that grandfather had been its first proud owner.

It just couldn't understand why Robert had forgotten all about his pencil box.

Well, Robert had been given a smart leather pencil case for his birthday, and it had a zip fastener. It was much more attractive than the old wooden pencil box.

All the other boys at the school admired it very much and kept pulling the zip to and fro, until in the end it broke.

'Oh, dear,' said Robert. 'Now I'll have to find my old wooden case again.'

Robert searched around in the toy cupboard and when he found the old pencil box he said: 'It's funny, but I think I like you best after all, and I shall always use you.'

The Lion and the Mouse

Once upon a time a little mouse was caught by a hungry lion. As the lion was about to eat him up, the little mouse said: 'Great lion, please let me go. I am only a little mouse. I am not going to make much of a meal for you to eat, anyway. If you let me go, some day I may be able to help you in return.'

'Perhaps you are right,' said the lion, releasing the mouse.

'Thank you,' said the little mouse as he ran off. 'You wait and see. One day you will be glad you let me go.'

Three days later, the lion was walking in the woods. Suddenly he found he had walked into a net that had been put there to trap him.

'Oh, get me out!' the lion roared in anger. 'Someone help me!'

'I can help you, mighty lion,' said the little mouse who had heard him calling. Immediately he started to bite the net with his sharp teeth and in no time at all the lion was free.

'Thank you little mouse,' the lion said gratefully. 'Thank you for getting me out of the net.'

And that is how the little mouse helped the lion, just as he promised he would.

Catch the Runaway Bull

The bull has escaped. Farmer Bill and his three farmhands are bravely trying to catch him again. Can you say which of the men has managed to get the rope around the bull's neck?

Matching Toys

Each of the large toys on the right has a small toy that belongs to it. Who can match the toys in pairs in the quickest time?

The Staffordshire Pair

Once there were two china dogs. They were known as the Staffordshire pair because that was the name of the place where they had been made. They were called Albert and Amelia.

Albert was white with brown patches on his ears and back. He was very handsome. His wife, Amelia, was much the same, only a little smaller. She was an extremely fine-looking china dog. Albert loved her dearly and she loved him faithfully in return.

They lived on the mantelpiece in an old country house, where they had lived for quite a hundred years or more. They could well remember gracious ladies moving about in long gowns and elegant gentlemen wearing high ruffled collars.

But now everything had changed. Their present mistress wore jeans and didn't like clutter. 'I'm going to get rid of a lot of these old bits and pieces!' she said – but fortunately Albert and Amelia weren't listening.

But there came the day when, to their great surprise, they were put on a table in the hall with a great many other things and the hall filled with people who started to buy the china on display. Albert and Amelia were quite shocked at the prospect of leaving their old home, but then a dreadful thing happened.

'I'll take the smallest of those two dogs. I don't want the other one,' someone said.

'Well, alright,' replied their mistress, and Amelia was removed from the table and packed in a box full of straw.

Poor Albert, he was so sad to be separated from Amelia. No-one bought him, so he was gathered up with the other unsold pieces of china and put away up in the attic.

As for Amelia, she was soon unpacked and placed proudly on the mantelpiece in a cosy cottage parlour, all by herself, next to a clock. Poor Amelia was so lonely and sad, and worried about Albert.

And so things might have continued if the old lady's husband had not enquired: 'Where's the other dog? Don't you think it would look better if we had the pair of them on the mantelpiece?'

The old lady agreed with her husband, and Amelia's heart leapt for joy – but then she realised that if somebody else had bought Albert they wouldn't know where to find him. But all went well. The old lady's husband soon found his way back to the old country house and Albert was swiftly packed into another box full of straw. As the lid closed he heard the old man say:

'My old wife is wonderful really, but

hasn't a clue over some things. Fancy parting a Staffordshire pair! Never mind, we'll soon put that right.'

Albert's heart beat with excitement – and when his new master took him out of the box and placed him on the mantelpiece beside his beloved Amelia he was beside himself with joy.

Now both dogs were happy once more, and where they belonged – together again.

'There now,' said the old man to his wife, 'a pair of proper beauties, they are!'

MIXED-UP MASKS

These six masks have got mixed up. See how quickly you can match the halves correctly to make an Indian Chief, an Indian Brave, a Cowboy, a Mexican, a Trapper and a Trooper.

Pirate's Puzzle

Pedro the pirate is puzzled. He can't decide if the sides of the square are straight or bent. Can you?

To the Rescue

The princess in the tower waits so patiently. Until the prince arrives and tries to set her free. Can you help him get to the princess?

Rosalie

The lake lies in a hollow in the hills. There are days when it is like a blue mirror and there are days when it rages like a whirlpool. Rosalie and her father, a fisherman, dwelt on its shores. They lived frugally. Sometimes they caught many fish, but other times they returned home with empty nets. When this happened, the fisherman would whisper, 'The Water Prince is in a bad mood.'

Rosalie grew curious and asked her father what the Prince was like.

'He is strong and handsome and has lived in the lake for a thousand years,' the fisherman replied. 'But say no more, for it is dangerous to speak of him.'

But this did not satisfy Rosalie. Secretly one night, when her father was not at home, she rowed to the deepest part of the lake and called again and again for the Water Prince to come to her.

Suddenly he appeared from the dark water. 'Here I am, Rosalie,' he said. But the girl was so overcome by his beauty that she could not speak. In an instant she fell in love with him, and their lips met in a tender kiss.

She said nothing to her father of this meeting, and the old man marvelled at how his boat was full of fish every day. He did not know that Rosalie returned many times to the Water Prince or that the full nets were the Prince's gift.

But one day something very strange happened. The fisherman woke one morning to find that Rosalie and his boat had gone. He searched beside the lake and was startled to see his boat arrive at the shore with no-one in it, and filled to the brim with fish.

He emptied the boat and rowed across the lake, looking for Rosalie. He feared the worst, but as he stared into the waters, out of the depths came Rosalie's sweet face, and she stretched out her hands to touch him. After that he was no longer sad. 'My Rosalie is alive,' he said. 'She lives beneath the lake with the Water Prince.' Some people thought he was mad, but others wondered why his nets were always full.

The Clever Deer

Once upon a time, there was a little deer who lived in a forest.

He had horns on his head and white spots on his back, like every other little deer. This little deer was not very strong, but he was clever.

In the forest there also lived a tiger, a fox, a rabbit and many other animals.

The rabbit was a good friend of the little deer. They played together almost every day. But the tiger was nobody's friend. He was much bigger and stronger than the little deer. He could have easily eaten him up if he had wanted to. Luckily for the deer, the tiger was foolish.

One day when the little deer was all alone, the tiger came along. The deer was very frightened but he said to himself, 'Here is the big, strong tiger. He can eat me up. What shall I do to keep him from eating me?'

But the tiger did not think of eating up the little deer. In fact, he had never seen a deer before.

'What are you?' the tiger asked.

'I am a little deer,' said the little deer.

'What are those things on your head?' asked the tiger.

'Those are horns,' said the little deer.

'Horns? What are horns for?' asked the tiger.

'Why, don't you know?' said the clever little deer. 'Horns are to kill tigers with.'

'Really?' said the foolish tiger. He began to be a little afraid. 'And why is your back all covered with white spots?'

'Don't you know?' said the clever little deer. 'Why, every time I eat a tiger I get a new white spot on my back.'

The foolish tiger did not know that the clever little deer was fooling him. He saw that the little deer's back was all covered with white spots.

'He must have eaten many tigers,' the

tiger said to himself. And he became so afraid that he ran away. The next animal he met was a fox, and the tiger told him all about the little deer. He told the fox about all the tigers the little deer must have eaten.

When the fox heard this, he laughed and he laughed.

'Oh, how foolish you are!' he said. 'How the clever little deer fooled you! You are so much bigger and stronger than he is. You could eat him up if you wanted to. He just told you those things to make you run away!'

'Really?' said the tiger.

'Come with me,' said the fox. 'I will show you. Just take me to the little deer.'

The fox got on the tiger's back and the tiger carried him to the little deer.

When the little deer saw the tiger coming back with the fox, he guessed why. But he was very clever.

'Hello, fox!' he called. 'I see you have kept your promise. You told me you would bring a nice, big tiger for me to eat. That is a very nice big tiger you have with you now. Thank you. Thank you very much!'

When the foolish tiger heard this, he was afraid. He was so afraid that he ran away before the fox could say a word. In fact the tiger ran so far away that the fox, the little deer and all the other animals of the forest never saw him again.

Sammy's New Coat

Sammy the puppy had caught a cold and had to stay indoors by the fire.

Wendy and John were upset, because they had planned to go for a lovely long

walk in the country. Now mummy said that Sammy must stay in and keep warm.

So off they went on their own. They wore their thick winter coats and woolly scarves because it had been snowing hard all night. They had great fun playing snowballs, but Wendy said it would have been much nicer if they could have taken Sammy with them.

The next day Sammy was a lot better, but mummy was still worried about him going out into the snow. 'I wouldn't mind, if he had a good thick coat to put on,' she said.

'I know what we can do,' cried Wendy. 'Wait a minute!'

She ran quickly to her dolls' pram and pulled out an old blue baby's coat. 'This is too big for any of my dolls,' she said. 'Sammy can wear it.'

'We will try it on him and see if he likes it,' said mummy – and she cut out the sleeves so that he would be more comfortable. Then Wendy buttoned it round his stomach. It fitted him perfectly and he seemed very pleased with it.

Now mummy was happy enough to let him go out in the cold, so off he went with the children to romp around and have a lovely game in the snow.

THE ENTERTAINERS

All the entertainers in the circus will be unable to do their acts until they have been given the right props. Can you decide which object each of them needs from the selection of props shown in the middle of the picture. Quick – the show is about to start!

Hunt For The Fox

Tallyho! Tallyho!
Hark to the horn,
Jump over hedges,
Gallop through corn.
The hunt is up,
The huntsmen ride,
The cunning fox
Has to hide.
The hounds sniff
Around the tree.
Is he there?
Can you see?

A milkmaid was on her way to market. On her head she was carrying a pail of milk, which she was going to sell.

As she walked, she said to herself, 'When I sell the milk at the market, I will get some money. With that money I will buy some eggs.

'From the eggs will come some chicks. I will keep these chicks until they are chickens. When the chickens are big, I will sell them at the market.

'When I sell the chickens at the market, I will get some money. With that money, I will buy a pretty red dress.

'When I wear that red dress, I will look very pretty. I will look so pretty that all the boys will want to marry me.

'But I will be very proud. I will say "No" to all of them. And I will shake my head like this.'

When the milkmaid shook her head, the pail of milk fell down. All the milk spilled over the ground.

Now the milkmaid had no milk to sell at the market.

Without the milk to sell, she would have no money to buy eggs.

Without eggs, she would have no chicks.

Without chicks, she would have no chickens to sell at the market.

Without chickens to sell at the market, she would have no money to buy a dress.

And all that because she shook her head! Poor milkmaid! That is what she got for being so proud.

INVISIBLE VISITORS

The toucans are gathered in the jungle. But while they are happily chatting they have failed to notice they have a number of silent visitors! If you look very carefully, you should be able to find several snakes hidden in the trees. How many can you see?

Mother's Mix-up

Something seems
To have gone wrong!
To which mother
Does each child belong?

The Grateful Pony

Jean and Michael were walking over the moors near their farm, when they came across a mother pony and her baby.

'Look, the mother is upset,' cried Jean. 'And no wonder. Her baby is trapped in the mud at the edge of that pond.' They crossed the rough grass to get closer to the animals and could clearly see that the young pony was unable to move a step and that the mother was quite powerless to help him.

'We will soon get him out,' said Michael, and he slipped off his shoes and paddled into the water's edge. 'I'll push, if you pull, Jean,' he called out. 'Are you ready – push now!'

With their help the baby pony was soon on dry land again. His mother licked him all over to make sure he was alright. 'That's marvellous,'. said Jean, 'there's nothing wrong with him.'

Jean and Michael led the two ponies away from the pond, then they trotted off across the moors

It wasn't long before a mist blew up.

'We must get back at once, Jean,' called out Michael – but that was easier said than done. They soon lost their way in the fog and Jean grew so tired of stumbling over the tussocks of grass that after a while she had to sit down and rest.

Michael, who knew they were completely lost, was wondering what they should do, when out of the white mist appeared two silhouettes. As they came closer, Jean exclaimed: 'Why, it is the mother pony and her baby!'

The animals came right over to the children as if they knew they were in trouble and needed help. 'I think they can show us the way. You ride on the mother pony, Jean,' Michael suggested.

The mother pony knew the way very well. She took them through the mist right to the edge of the farm. 'How wonderful,' said Jean.

'We helped them and now they have helped us,' smiled Michael.

The Three Wishes

Once upon a time, there was a poor man named Sven. Sven lived in a little cottage with his wife, Eda.

Every day, Sven went to chop wood in the forest. This was the way he made his living. But he did not earn much money. Many times he and his wife, Eda, were very hungry.

One day, when Sven was in the forest, he cried out, 'Oh, my! How hungry I am! I only wish I had some money.'

Suddenly, a beautiful fairy appeared before him. First, she touched him lightly with her wand. Then she said, 'Dear Sven, your troubles are over. I will help you. I give you three wishes. Whatever you wish will come true.'

Then, just as suddenly, she disappeared.

Sven hurried home. He told his wife, Eda, about their good luck. They both danced with joy. Then they both sat down to talk things over. They began to wonder what they should wish for.

After a while, Sven and Eda began to feel hungry. It was dinner time, so they sat down at the table.

'My dear wife,' said Sven, 'I am very hungry. Please give me something to eat. While we eat we can talk about the three wishes.'

'I think,' said Eda, 'we should ask to be rich.'

'Ah,' said Sven, 'we should ask for a beautiful house.'

'Ah,' cried Eda, 'we could even ask for a castle. Or perhaps I will ask for gold and silver and everything else I have ever wanted.'

'Why not ask for a big family?' said Sven. 'Given my choice, I should like to have six boys and six girls.'

'Not me,' said Eda. 'I would like three boys and nine girls.'

And so the husband and wife continued. They kept talking and wondering what their wishes should be.

Then Sven looked at his dinner plate. It was empty and he was so very hungry!

'Oh,' he said, 'I am half starved. I wish I had a great big sausage for my dinner.' Thereupon a great big sausage appeared on Sven's plate. Eda was very angry.

'Oh Sven,' she cried, 'you have been very foolish. Now you have used up one of our wishes. There are only two wishes left.' Sven agreed that he had been very foolish. 'But we can still ask for a castle,' he said, 'and a large family.'

'No,' said Eda. 'If we only have two wishes I want a castle first, then diamonds and pearls.' Eda kept on talking and complaining until Sven could stand it no more and he began to lose his temper.

'Stop your complaining!' he cried out. 'I wish that sausage were stuck to your nose!' Thereupon the sausage jumped in the air and attached itself to the end of Eda's nose! The poor woman was very surprised, and so was Sven. They knew Sven had wasted another wish.

'We can still ask for great riches,' suggested Sven.

'But what good will all the riches in the world do? Now I have to go around looking foolish with a sausage stuck on the end of my nose!'

'Oh, I wish I had never seen that sausage, and I wish never to see it again!' cried out Sven.

Eda touched her nose – the sausage was gone and Sven and Eda were just as poor as they had ever been. They had used up the three wishes that the kind fairy had given them. But they had no riches, no pearls, no diamonds, no castle, and no large family – they did not even have a sausage for their dinner!

Search around the Shipwreck

Here are two skin-divers looking for shells for their collection. But they can't find any! Can you spot the twelve different types of shell the artist has cleverly tucked away in this picture of an underwater shipwreck?

The *W*ind and the Sun

Once upon a time the wind and the sun were talking. The sun said that the wind was too cruel. But the wind said that the sun was too kind.

'I have to be cruel to be strong,' said the wind. 'I am stronger than you.'

They talked and they talked. But they could not agree. After they had been talking a long time, they saw a man coming down the road.

'Now we will see who is stronger,' the sun said. 'Let us agree that the one who can make that man take off his coat is the stronger.' The wind agreed. 'You begin,' said the sun to the wind.

The sun hid behind a cloud, and the wind began to blow. The wind blew and blew. But the stronger the wind blew, the colder the man felt. So he would not take off his coat.

By and by, the wind had to give up. 'Now it is your turn,' he said to the sun.

The sun came out and shone upon the man, while the wind was still.

'How nice it is now,' said the man, and he opened his coat.

The sun shone down, stronger and stronger. Soon it was so warm that the man took off his coat.

'You see,' said the sun to the wind, 'kindness works better than cruelty.'

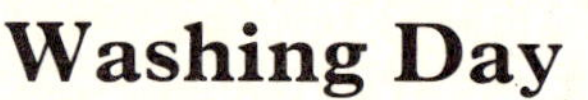

Washing Day

'Rub and scrub,'
Sings Caroline,
'I'll hang my clothes
Upon the line.

'And since the sun
Is in the sky,
It won't be long
Before they dry.'

But Mr Wind
Likes washing day,
And loves to blow
The clothes away.

Tea Time

Jane sets the table.
It is time for tea.
Says: 'There'll be four,
As well as me.'
Cup, saucer, plate
Each will get.
How many dishes
Must she set?

The Magic Hammer

Tinker Tim was coming down the lane, pushing his little barrow, when he found the village children outside the gate of their playground. They all looked rather sad and miserable.

'Hello, whatever is the matter?' asked Tinker Tim. 'You all look as if you had lost tenpence and found a ha'penny,' he joked.

'Our playground is locked up, Tim,' the children told him. 'We can't play any of the games we wanted to and now we shall have to go home.'

'Well, let me see what I can do,' said Tinker Tim, who was well known for being able to fix things. He searched around in his barrow, muttering: 'Let me find my magic hammer.'

It didn't take long for old Tim to find his toolbox, and inside was his funny little hammer.

'Now Jimmy,' he said to one of the little boys, who was pulling along a tiny wooden horse. 'Bring that over here and I'll give it three magic taps.'

Tap, tap, tap, went the hammer and Jimmy's eyes grew round with surprise.

'My horse is growing!' he gasped.

'Yes, that is my magic hammer working,' said Tinker Tim. 'It makes things grow bigger.' And the horse grew and grew until it was large enough for little Jimmy to ride on.

While Jimmy's two sisters helped him to climb onto the horse's back, Tim had another bright idea. He found a piece of flat tin in his barrow and after bending over the rough edges and one end of it, he laid it flat on the ground.

'It doesn't look much,' he said, 'but I think you boys and girls will have good fun with it.' Then, once again he used his magic hammer. Three taps and the tin grew, just as the horse had done.

'But we can't play with that,' said the children.

'That is because you haven't guessed what it is,' laughed Tim. 'Now, you watch. You'll soon see!'

He took the tin over to the playground gate and hung the bent end over the top bar so that it sloped down to the ground.

'Now, can you see what it is?' he asked. 'It's made a lovely giant slide for you all to play on.'

The children were absolutely delighted with Tim's idea and when he noticed that Jimmy's sister Clare was carrying a ruler, it gave him another idea.

'Lend me your ruler, Clare,' he asked, 'and I'll make something else for you.' He found a piece of twig, placed it on the ground and laid the ruler across the top of it. After three magic taps the ruler and the twig started to grow and straight away the children could see what this was meant to be. 'Why, it's a see-saw. Tinker Tim, how kind you are!'

After a few minutes all the children were busy enjoying themselves in their new magic-made playground.

'Thank you Tim,' they all shouted and waved as old Tinker Tim started to push his heavily laden barrow down the lane once more.

'Don't thank me, thank my little magic hammer,' he laughed. 'I hope you will all have a happy afternoon. Now I must get along and do some real work.' And he gave them one last wave before he turned the corner out of sight.

What do you see?

Take a quick look at this picture and decide what you think it is. When you look a second time, you might think it looks like something else. In fact, there are two pictures in one. Can you name them both?

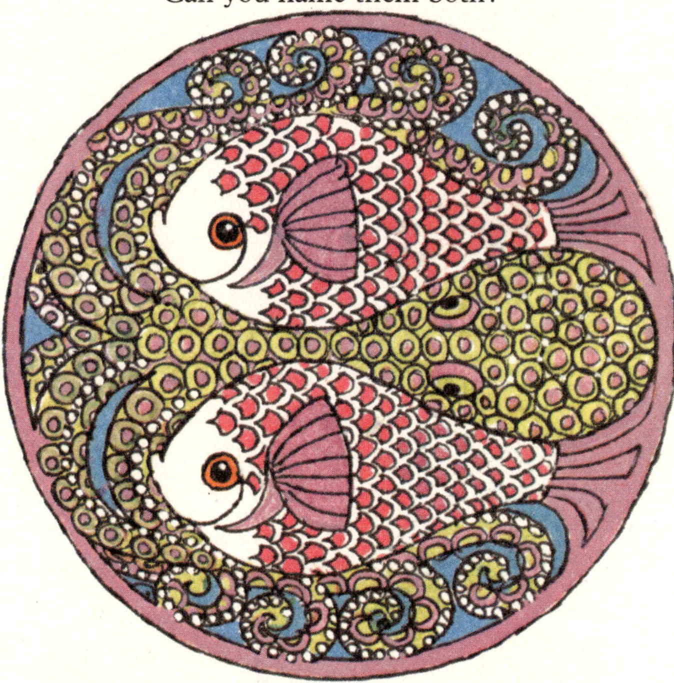

Tiger Twins

These four tigers are prowling around their enclosure. You may think they all look exactly alike, but only two of them have an identical pattern of stripes on their coats. Study the tigers carefully to find the tiger twins, Rajah and Samson.

Fancy Dress Party

What fun! Everyone at the birthday party has been asked to wear fancy dress. Five of the children have already arrived – a cowboy, a clown, a pirate, a bunny and a squaw. Which is the odd one out?

The Sunflower and the Violet

Once upon a time there were two flowers that lived side by side in a garden.

One flower was tall and splendid. It stood straight and high, its bright golden face turned to the sun and its leaves waving gently in the breeze. It was a giant sunflower.

The other flower was small and crouched in the shade of the sunflower. It was a pretty, deep violet colour but no-one ever noticed it hiding under the leaves of the tall flower. It was a violet.

The sunflower was proud and haughty. 'No-one will ever see you, you silly violet,' it would say, which would make the violet very unhappy. It knew the sunflower's words were true.

One day some children came to play in the garden. The violet watched them running about and laughing and throwing a ball to each other. What fun they were having! The violet felt happy just watching them.

Suddenly the ball the children were playing with came crashing across the flowerbed to stop beneath the sunflower, just beside the violet.

The children came running over to look for their ball and began searching amongst the flowers.

One little boy held the sunflower back. 'Here it is!' he cried, pointing to the ball.

'Oh look,' said a little girl, bending down beside the violet. 'What a pretty flower. I've never seen it before because it has been hidden. What a shame. Why don't we ask Daddy to put the sunflower somewhere else so that everyone can see the violet. This can be our own garden.'

And that is what happened.

The Fox and the Stork

Once upon a time a fox went up to a stork and said:

'Good morning, stork!'

'Good morning, fox! What news have you today?'

'I have been reading learned books and I understand that you and I are cousins. We should visit one another and make friends.'

'Fine,' said the stork. 'You must invite me to dinner.'

So the fox invited the stork to dinner. He cooked some porridge and put it on a plate and said to the stork:

'Help yourself, stork! Take as much as you want!'

The stork pecked away at the plate with his long beak, but couldn't pick up any of the porridge. And so the fox licked it all up himself.

The next day the stork invited the fox to dinner. He cooked some soup, poured it into a jug with a long narrow neck and said to the fox:

'Help yourself, fox! Take as much as you want!'

The fox walked round and round the jug, poked his nose in, but couldn't reach a drop of soup. So the stork, with his long beak, drank it all.

And that was the end of the friendship between the fox and the stork.

the clockwork train

The clockwork train runs round and round,
Six coaches it can take.
Three passengers in every coach,
How many does that make?

Musical Mix-Up

Bang! Tootle! Crash! These six musicians, all from different countries, are playing at once. What a hullaballoo, and the problem is even worse because the players have managed to get their instruments mixed up. Can you match the players to their correct instrument?

The Boy who loved Clocks

'Mother, mother. Have you heard the news? The king is giving a purse of gold to any of his people who can make a clock that will keep perfect time for a day and a night.'

Little Henry came racing in from the market square of the small French town in which he lived with his widowed mother. His father had been a clock maker and had taught his son all he knew about the trade.

'If I win, won't it be lovely?' said the boy, his eyes sparkling. 'We shall have plenty to eat then.'

'I hope you will,' said his mother, 'although I sometimes think it would be better for you to be apprenticed to old Simon, the blacksmith. People do not always want or need clocks, but there are always horses to be shod.'

But Henry had inherited his father's passion for clocks and was always working at them.

For two days the boy worked hard at engraving a new brass face for the clock he had just finished. Finally it was ready and, wrapping it in a scarf, he kissed his mother and set out for the palace.

Outside, he found old Simon waiting for him.

'I've come to wish you luck, Henry,' he said. 'And to give you some advice. I've heard that the king thinks he knows everything about clocks, since it is his favourite hobby. So, be wise and agree with everything the king says.'

Inside the palace Henry found a crowd of other clockmakers and they were all told to leave their clocks and return at the same time the next day. The time went slowly for Henry but when he arrived back at the palace the guard at the gate took him to the king's chamber at once.

There, on the table, stood his clock, ticking merrily away and still keeping perfect time. A few minutes later the king came in, followed closely by a servant carrying the purse of gold.

'Well, well – the winner is just a boy!' exclaimed the king in surprise. 'You may be young, but you are the best clockmaker. Only your clock kept proper time.'

Henry felt his face flush with delight, but then the king added:

'But there is one mistake. You have marked the figure four on the face by IV. That is wrong. You should have shown the figure with four strokes like this: IIII.'

It was on the tip of Henry's tongue to say he had done it the way his father had shown him, but then he remembered Simon's warning.

'Of course, your majesty,' he said. 'Shall I alter it?'

'By all means,' said the king, 'and I would like you to come to the palace to become the royal clockmaker.'

After that Henry became a very famous clockmaker, but he always showed the figure four the way the king had shown him. And if you look at a few clocks yourself you are bound to find that some of them are marked with the four strokes in the same manner.

King Bowlegs

'Catch that cat!' roared the king. 'Catch that big tabby. He's been after the royal goldfish.' With the portly king in the lead, everyone in the royal household chased the palace cat.

'I think I've got him,' cried the king, when the cat was finally trapped in a corner. But, alas, the clever tabby managed to escape once again. 'Oh, bother,' sighed the king, 'that always happens!'

The truth is, the tabby cat found it very easy to escape since he was able to dart straight between the old king's big bow-legs.

The king sighed again. 'Whoever heard of a king with bow-legs? How I wish I had long straight ones.'

At that moment, in rushed the Lord Chamberlain. 'Your Majesty! Your Majesty! The sentries report that a dragon is approaching the palace. Whatever are we to do?'

'Call out our brave young knights,' replied the king. 'They will soon settle one old dragon.'

'They are all away in the next kingdom, Your Majesty, trying to win the hand of the princess in marriage.'

'Oh, of course, I quite forgot,' said the king. 'Well, how about the court magician? Can he not cast a spell?'

'No, Your Majesty,' replied the Lord Chamberlain. 'He has gone with the young knights to try to help them with his magic. I am afraid you will have to do it yourself.'

'Oh, I say, must I?' stammered the king in alarm.

'Well, you are the king, you know,' answered the Lord Chamberlain, 'and you, of all people, should be able to set us all an example.'

So, the king knew he would have to fight the dragon himself and off he went on his old bow-legs to fight the foe.

Just as the king was passing through the palace orchard he heard the roar of the dragon's fiery breath. In a flash, he climbed the nearest apple tree, trying to hide himself amongst the leafy branches.

As it happened, the branch he chose to sit on was not very strong. Crack! It snapped just as the dragon was passing underneath. Down fell the old king, right onto the neck of the dragon. His bow-legs fitted perfectly round the dragon's scaly neck, and when he squeezed with his knees the dragon fell over in a faint for lack of air.

'Take him to the stables,' cried the king. 'Perhaps we can train him to be a household pet.'

After that the dragon became the king's favourite pet, and because the king had bow-legs he was the only person in the royal household who could ride him. And that made him feel very important indeed – and it also meant he was a lot happier about having bow-legs.

The Race

A fox was running along the banks of a river and saw a carp lying in the shallows. It lay there in the mud without moving.

The fox said:

'Hello, carp! They say you don't know how to run. Is it true?'

'Oh, no, Mr. Fox, I can run as fast as you,' said the carp.

'I don't believe it.'

'Then let's take a bet on it!'

So the fox and the carp had a bet as to who would reach the mouth of the river first. The fox was to run along the river bank and the carp in the river. The carp, however, was lazy and had no desire to race. He told the carp lying beside him about the bet with the fox, the second carp told his neighbour, and so on until in a short while all the carp in the river knew about it. And there were a great many of them.

The fox ran along beside the river, and after a while, called out:

'Carp, are you there?'

And the nearest carp in the river answered:

'Here I am.'

The fox ran even faster and, after a while, called out again:

'Carp, are you there?'

Again the nearest carp in the river answered:

'Here I am.'

The fox now ran like the wind, and as the river was very winding, he took short cuts wherever possible. But to no avail. Whenever he called out, one of the carp always answered:

'Here I am.'

When he finally reached the mouth of the river, he called out for the last time:

'Carp, are you there?'

And the last carp, which was lazily resting in the mud, replied:

'Here I am, fox, but my, what a time you took!'

And from that day a fox has never spoken to a fish.

Valiant Adventurers

The artist has drawn four valiant adventurers, each of whom set out on their voyages at different times in history. The first is a Viking, off to conquer fresh lands, the second is an astronaut, the third a brave knight, and last of all there is an arctic explorer. Match each of them with their correct transport.

MIDSUMMER DAY

These four peasant girls are having fun dancing to folk music. They are celebrating with a traditional dance for Midsummer Day, twirling round the pole, crossing their ribbons as they pass one another. One of the girls' ribbons has come away from the pole. To which dancer does it belong?

Gilbert and the Birds

Gilbert glider was so tired of having his wings bent.

'That silly boy doesn't know how to fly me,' he grumbled. 'He puts my wings on crooked and down I crash. Oh dear, here I go again!'

Gilbert was lucky this time. He landed in a patch of long grass.

'I wish I were a bird!' he sighed.

'Why don't you come and live with us, then?' asked a hedge-sparrow.

'If only I could,' said Gilbert. 'I would love to be able to fly the way you do.'

'We'll teach you,' said the hedge-sparrow. 'Next time that silly boys throws you into the air, try to steer for the wood.'

The boy soon found Gilbert in the long grass, and straightened his bent wings. He carried him to the middle of the meadow and gave him a good push.

'Now, steer for the wood!' cried the hedge-sparrow, close beside Gilbert.

'I will help,' said the north wind, and he puffed his hardest. Soon Gilbert was skimming along with the wind, and after a few minutes he reached the wood. He landed on the top of a very tall tree.

'Well done!' said the hedge-sparrow. 'Now I will teach you to fly properly. First, you flap your wings – like this.'

Gilbert tried to do the same but just could not manage it.

'Never mind,' said the hedge-sparrow patiently. 'You can learn to build a nest first. First you must find some twigs . . .'

'I don't think I want to build a nest, thank you,' said Gilbert.

'Dear me!' said the hedge-sparrow. 'If you cannot flap your wings, and you don't want to build a nest, I really don't think we shall ever make a bird of you,' he sighed and flew away.

Poor Gilbert. There he was, all alone on the top of the tree.

Presently along came the little boy to look for him. There was a bigger boy with him this time.

'Here I am,' said Gilbert, but the boys didn't hear him.

'I will help you,' said the north wind. 'Shake yourself!'

Gilbert shook and shook, the north wind blew. Down flew Gilbert into the meadow and the boys soon spotted him. Gilbert was so happy!

Then the big boy showed the little boy how to fix the wings on, so that Gilbert could fly properly.

'Who wants to be a bird?' he said to himself, as he glided through the air.

DOUBLE TAKE

Two old ladies with bows in their hair.
Turn the book round and see who hides there.

Carousel Cavalcade

Five carousel horses are prancing up and down on the large fairground roundabout. Only two of the horses are exactly the same. Can you spot them?

Match the Mermaids

Look carefully at the four merry mermaids and also at their shadows. You will find only three match. Find the mermaid who doesn't match her shadow.

The Runaway Wheel

The little brown cart went chugging along,
Taking the eggs from the farm,
When one of its wheels went rolling away,
And the farmer jumped out in alarm!

The wheel gathered speed as it rolled downhill,
And crashed through the farmyard with glee;
The neighbours rushed out from their houses nearby,
Oh, my! What a sight they did see.

Ducklings and turkeys, goslings and geese,
Went flying all over the place,
And the wheel carried on at a terrible speed,
Till it crashed and fell flat on its face.

The farmer then caught it – he gave it a spank,
And carried it back on his head.
But the little wheel winked to the little brown cart –
'Boy, that was a fine spin!' he said.

THE SNOWMAN

There was once a little old woman who lived all by herself in a little cottage in the woods. She was very lonely, for no-one ever came to see her. One winter night the snow fell very heavily, and the little old woman woke up next day to find the whole world was white.

'I'll make a snowman,' she thought, 'and then I needn't be lonely any more.'

She set to work with her spade and soon she had made a fine snowman. Then she put an old hat on the snowman's head and a scarf round his neck, and then he was finished.

All this digging had made her very hungry, so she went to make her lunch.

While she was away the snowman decided to go for a walk. Soon he met a little old man.

'That's a very fine hat you are wearing,' said the little old man. 'I haven't a hat and my head feels very cold.'

The snowman felt sorry for him.

'Would you like my hat?' he asked. 'My head never feels the cold because, as you can see, I'm a snowman.'

The little old man took the hat gladly.

'That's a very fine scarf you are wearing,' he said. 'I haven't a scarf to wear, and my neck does get so cold.'

Again the snowman felt sorry for him.

'Well, would you like my scarf, as well?' he asked. 'My neck never feels cold. It's because I'm a snowman.'

So the little old man wound the scarf round his neck, too. Then he raised his new hat to the snowman and went on his way.

Soon the sun began to shine and the snowman just melted away.

The little old woman was very upset when she saw that the snowman had gone. She ran to the gate and looked up and down the road. Then she saw the little old man coming towards her.

'Have you seen a snowman?' she asked, and then she noticed the scarf. 'Oh, that's the scarf he was wearing,' she said. '*You* must be the snowman!'

After that the little old man and the little old woman were married and lived happily together in the cottage, and the little old woman was never lonely again.

Firework Night

It's Firework Night once again. Everyone is wrapped up warmly against the cold night air, but they are enjoying the warmth from the bonfire and admiring the fireworks that seem to be exploding in all directions in the sky. This is a counting game. See how many blue and white stars there are in the sky, how many sparklers the children are holding, how many people there are at the bonfire party.

A LUCKY GAME

Billy had been given a lovely cricket bat for his birthday. He was so keen to try it out that he said to his sister, Julie: 'Come on, let's have a game straight away.'

'But don't you think our garden is rather small to play cricket in?' said Julie.

'Yes, but at least we can try,' said Billy as he rushed outside.

It was a great shame, but the first time Julie bowled to him, he hit the ball so hard that it went straight over the garden fence and into the garden of Mr Miggs, who lived next door. Mr Miggs was not very fond of children and definitely would not want them in his garden.

'Oh dear! What shall we do?' sighed Billy. He peered over the fence and there was the ball, right in the middle of the lawn.

'Do you think Mr Miggs would notice if I jumped over and got the ball back?' Billy asked Julie.

'Well, do be quick. I haven't seen him around this morning,' said Julie, 'so, with any luck, he could be out.'

Billy checked again – there was still no sign of Mr Miggs – and he was over the fence in a moment. He ran across the lawn, but just as he picked up the ball he noticed a plume of smoke drifting up into the air at the bottom of Mr Migg's garden.

'I'd better see what it is,' Billy decided. He ran down the garden only to discover that the garden shed was on fire. It was only a small fire at the moment, but Billy realised it would soon get worse if he didn't act swiftly.

'Mr Migg's garden shed is on fire!' he called out to Julie, as he ran back to where she was standing waiting for him. 'It'll burn the shed down in no time!'

'You had better find the hosepipe, Billy,' said Julie. 'I'll come over and help you.'

Together they found the hose, fixed it to the garden tap and directed the jet of water through the garden shed door.

They held it steady for quite a few minutes before the smoke and flames began to go out. Just at that moment Mr Miggs arrived and ran down the garden towards the children.

'Goodness!' he exclaimed. 'My shed is on fire! Thank you so much for helping, children!'

Mr Miggs took over from Billy and Julie and sprayed the shed all over to make absolutely sure the fire was quite finished.

'I am so grateful to you both,' Mr Miggs smiled. 'How lucky you saw the smoke.'

At this point Billy thought he had better explain why he had been in Mr Miggs' garden in the first place. Mr Miggs laughed – he realised they were both sensible and said that since his garden was so much bigger than theirs they would be welcome to play in it any time they wanted.

Billy and Julie were so pleased. Billy's birthday game of cricket had turned out to be a lucky game.

THINGS WE NEED

This game is all about 'relationships'. Things we need in everyday life are mixed up with the things they come from. Work out the relationships and match the pairs.

Faithful Beauty

There was only one horse left in the stable at Hubert's farm. Her name was Beauty. All the other horses had gone.

The farmer used tractors and big lorries on the farm instead of horses.

Beauty was the only horse left, and she was going away the next day. But that night, Irma, the farmer's little daughter, fell gravely ill. The farmer rushed off to get the doctor.

'I'll take my new car,' he thought. But when he flung himself into the driver's seat he could not get it started, no matter how hard he tried. In despair, he cried, 'What can I do? I must get the doctor quickly!'

Suddenly he remembered Beauty, the faithful horse in the stable. Beauty neighed when she saw the farmer, and he led her out into the yard and harnessed her to the trap and set off at once. It was as if Beauty knew that Irma was in danger, for she galloped every inch of the way through the quiet lanes and darkened streets to the doctor's surgery. When she had taken the farmer and the doctor back to the farm, Beauty was trembling and sweating with the great effort she had made.

As the sun rose, little Irma lay sleeping peacefully, on the way to recovery, saved by the doctor's skill.

'You're a good friend,' said farmer Hubert gratefully, rubbing Beauty down. 'You're staying with us for good now. What would have happened to our little Irma if you hadn't been here?'

Beauty neighed and rubbed her head against the farmer's rough jacket. She felt happy. She felt wanted again.

Witches

Twelve witches stealing through the night
With turnip lanterns glowing bright;
Each turnip shared by witches three
How many lanterns will there be?

The Orchard

In the orchard I can see
Fruit on every apple tree.
Twelve rows standing in the sun
Twenty trees in every one.
Now, you must tell me,
The total sum of apple trees?

A Musical Family

My father plays the cello,
My mother plays the lute,
My sister plays the violin,
And I can play the flute,
You'll soon find without a doubt,
Which instrument is the odd one out.

The Oyster Catcher

One hundred little oysters
Were lying in the sea,
A diver came and found them
And took home twenty three.
How many little oysters lay
In the sea for another day?

THE GRATEFUL BEAR

The land is all ice and snow in Greenland, where Nika and Jolo lived with their parents in an igloo. Eskimo children help their mother and father from a very early age, and every day these two children cut a hole in the ice so that they could catch fish. One day they were fishing when they saw some hunters catch a mother polar bear.

'Look,' cried Nika, 'the baby bear has hidden in a cave.' The hunters had not seen the tiny bear crawl away, and when they had gone the two children went into the cave to find it.

'What a handful!' laughed Nika as the woolly bundle growled at her and tried to escape from her arms.

'But so pretty,' smiled Jolo, watching the baby bear's antics.

Their father agreed to let them keep the bear as a pet. 'But only until he grows big enough to be killed for food,' he added. This made the children sad, but they knew that food was scarce in their land, and that their father was right. After all, the bear would be fed with fish and seal meat that they really needed for themselves. Just the same, Burri-Burri, which was the name they gave him, became great friends with Nika and Jolo. They played together and rolled about in the snow, and all the time the bear grew bigger, too! At last the children's father spoke. 'I must slaughter your bear to-morrow,' he announced. And their mother got the pots ready for cooking.

But the next morning, when Nika and Jolo went outside their igloo, they found their beloved bear had broken loose and run away.

'Perhaps he will come back,' said Jolo. Their father grumbled at losing a month's supply of meat.

However, Burri-Burri was soon forgotton until one night . . .

'What's that noise?' Jolo whispered to Nika.

'I don't know,' she answered. She, too, had woken suddenly. Quietly, so as not to wake their parents, the children slipped outside the igloo, and there was Burri-Burri padding round the hut. They were so happy they hugged him. Then they gave him some fish and soon he went away. Every day after that they saved a scrap of blubber or fish from their meals and left the food out for Burri-Burri.

They were delighted when they rushed out each morning and found that the bear had accepted their gift, but they were careful to clear up all traces of what they had done, for their father was still angry at the bear's disappearance and would have been cross with them. However, even Burri-Burri's secret visits stopped after a while, and the boy and the girl thought that he must have gone for good.

A year passed, and Nika and Jolo were once again fishing through a hole in the ice. They even hoped to catch a seal. Sometimes seals poke their heads through a hole for air, and if a hunter is very quick, he can catch one before it dives under the water again. The children were so excited that they did not notice a blizzard was on the way, and they were caught in it before they knew what was happening.

Quickly they dug themselves a snow hole and took shelter in it. For two whole days, until the blizzard was over, they stayed there. At last they were able to crawl out, but when they looked around, they were in despair. The snow had changed everything; it had made new hills and valleys. They seemed to be in a country they had never seen before.

'How shall we find our way home?' Nika asked tearfully.

'We'll be all right,' Jolo said bravely to his sister, although he knew they might get lost and freeze to death.

'I'm hungry,' Nika said. To make matters worse, a heavy cloud covered the sun, and made the day dark.

Jolo and Nika began to walk into the unknown. There was a thick mist now, which made it hard to see ahead, and they made slow progress. Presently, to their horror, they heard the hoarse and terrifying growl of a polar bear.

They clutched each other tightly. 'Don't be afraid,' Jolo whispered, trying not to show his own fear, as the growls grew louder. Then the huge shape of a bear looked out of the mist, so near they could see his fangs. The two children were in terrible danger. But, at that moment, the animal began to whimper, stretching his paws out to them.

'It's Burri-Burri!' cried Nika, and with joy and relief the children hugged their old friend, before following him all the way home. Near their igloo, he left them, knowing they were safe – then he lumbered away into the distance. But Nika and Jolo knew that was not the last they had seen of their dear friend.

Picnic Packing

Here is a picture of a picnic basket, crammed with good things to eat. Mummy is just going over her list – look carefully and check your list against hers. You should find twelve different items.

Indian Signals

See the Indian signals
Rising in the sky.
Would you like to read them?
It's easy if you try.
One puff makes A,
Two puffs make B,
Continue in this way –
If you count up carefully
You'll soon know what they say.

Easter Parade

Here are five ladies wearing splendid hats, entering the Easter Parade. All of them deserve a prize, but the object of this puzzle is to decide which is the hat with a real difference from the others.

The Proud Princess

Once upon a time there was a beautiful princess. She was so proud that she refused to marry any of her suitors.

'I intend to wed only the richest, most handsome man in the land,' she said, as she faced the last of her suitors.

He was so angry that, as he turned away, he muttered a magic spell and immediately the beautiful princess was turned into an ugly maid.

After that no more suitors came, and in the end she was glad enough to accept the hand of the palace's new swineherd.

The spoilt princess now had to do all the dirty work; peeling potatoes, cleaning the pig-sty, and washing her husband's dirty clothes. And very often she wept silently.

But, as time passed, she noticed that the swineherd had a kind heart, gentle eyes, and a friendly voice.

One evening she said to him, 'Forgive me. I have been a proud, silly woman. All I want now is to be a good wife.'

Immediately the evil spell was broken. She became even more beautiful than before; the swineherd became changed into a handsome prince; and the two of them lived happily ever after in his magnificent castle.

The Magic Crystal

Once upon a time, in an ancient country near Turkey, there lived a wise Sultan who ruled over many thousands of people. He had three good and clever sons: Ali, the eldest, Ben, the second son, and Cyrip, the youngest.

One day the Sultan called his sons to him and said, 'I am growing old and would like to live the rest of my life quietly and at peace. I want each of you to go out into the world, and he who returns with the secret of a happy nation will take my place on the throne.'

The three young men ventured forth, and each returned to the palace at the end of the year, certain that he had found the secret of a happy nation. In the Room of the Golden Throne they met up with each other for it was here they were to show their father what they had brought back.

Ali began. Pulling a leather purse from his travelling bag, he said: 'This is a magic purse. It will always be full of gold for the ruler of a country. If I were Sultan I would never have any subjects who were poor and hungry, for my purse would always provide for their needs. What nation could be happier?'

Ali had hardly finished when Ben eagerly brought out what he had found. 'Look!' he cried. 'I have a magic arrow.'

'What good is that?' asked his father doubtfully.

'In time of war,' Ben replied, 'it will kill all soldiers who fight against us. A nation is surely happy that needn't fear its enemies.'

Now it was young Cyrip's turn, but he felt that what he had found could not compare with the secrets of his brothers. His father insisted, however, and Cyrip drew forth a small crystal ball. 'It's nothing much,' he said. 'It won't make gold and it won't kill our enemies.'

'Well, what use is it?' his brothers demanded.

'Whoever looks into it knows right and wrong,' he said. 'No wicked person, though he be the highest in the land, can hide from its owner; and no good person, though he be the poorest of the poor, can ever be unjustly treated.'

At this, the Sultan led Cyrip to the throne. 'You are my successor,' he announced. 'You will rule with your magic crystal. What nation can be as happy as one that knows justice.'

The Giant Snake

A giant snake lived in the hot African jungle. She stole the chickens and pigs of the village, but she was so powerful that the hunters were much too afraid to go anywhere near her.

Even the spells of the witchdoctor would not work against her. But Kima, a clever boy of the village, had a plan. 'I will catch that snake,' he told himself. Secretly he gathered bamboo from the jungle.

With the sticks, he built a cage with bars just far enough apart to let the snake through. When the cage was finished he took a young pig from his father's sty and shut it in the cage. The snake smelled the pig, slid between the bars and swallowed it whole.

But when she tried to get out of the cage, she got stuck, for she was now as fat as the pig she had eaten! Kima had caught the snake.

No wonder clever little Kima is now the village hero.

Young John, Old John

This is the story of John, young and old. When John was small, everyone called him Johnny. He was such a dear little boy! His parents spoilt him as much as they could, and Johnny did exactly as he liked.

When Johnny was old enough for school he didn't want to go, so he didn't go! When the other children went off to their lessons every morning, little Johnny went out fishing or chasing butterflies. He had lots of fun.

He thought the other children were stupid to go to school, and when they did their homework he poked fun at them.

But as he grew up, Johnny began to be ashamed that he could not read, write or count – but now it was too late.

He sat with a book pretending to read, but people knew it was only pretence. As time passed he changed from young Johnny to old John.

'Ha, Ha, old John can't read,' shouted the children. And, oh, how old John wished he could!

Four Seasons

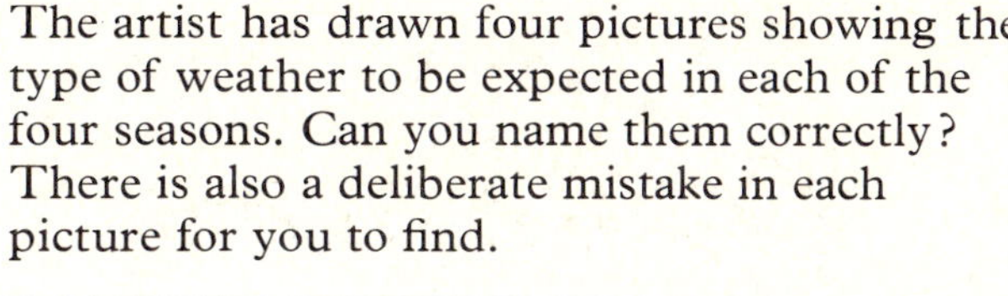

The artist has drawn four pictures showing the type of weather to be expected in each of the four seasons. Can you name them correctly? There is also a deliberate mistake in each picture for you to find.

a

b

c

d

SNOWFLAKE PATTERNS

Here are three groups of snowflakes. Each group pattern is made up of individual snowflake patterns, except that in each case one snowflake is different from the others.

The Unwanted Witch

'Nobody seems to need a witch these days,' thought Hazel sadly, as she ironed her old black cloak.

Ever since she had lost her job at the palace, Witch Hazel had lived alone with Sooty, her little black cat.

'I might still have been the Royal Witch if I hadn't made such a mess of my spells,' thought Hazel.

Suddenly the kitchen was filled with the smell of something burning.

'Thunder and lightning!' cried the old witch, gazing at the hole which she had just burned in her cloak.

Witch Hazel didn't know a single spell for mending clothes, so she had to take out her work basket and cover the hole with a bright green patch.

'Of course, if I got a new job,' she thought hopefully, 'I could always buy myself a new cloak.'

Later that day, Witch Hazel was out shopping when she almost tripped over Mr Black the chimney sweep, and his ladder.

'Good afternoon, Mr Black,' said Hazel.

'I really don't know what's good about it,' sighed the old chimney sweep. 'I'm so tired and my legs are much too wobbly to be climbing any more ladders today.'

'Could I help you?' asked Hazel, feeling very sorry for the old sweep.

'Are you any good at sweeping chimneys, Hazel?' Mr Black asked eagerly.

Witch Hazel had never swept a chimney before, but she felt she had to help him somehow.

While Mr Black looked on in amazement, Hazel crossed her fingers for luck and chanted a spell.

'Broomstick down the chimney fly
In the twinkling of an eye,
By brightest day
By blackest night
Sweep every speck of soot in sight.'

The broomstick went to work and in seconds the chimney was beautifully clean.

Witch Hazel was as delighted as the old chimney sweep, for at last she had made a spell that had actually worked!

Mr Black then and there gave Hazel the job of assistant chimney sweep.

So, if you should see a witch wearing a cloak with a bright green patch you'll know that's Hazel – the fastest chimney sweep in town!

The Football Team

Here are the boys in the football team, lined up before the match starts. They are all proudly wearing their team colours – except one boy who isn't dressed correctly. Which one is he?

DAISY CHAIN

The lawn is a mass of daisies and Kitty is having a lovely afternoon sitting in the spring sunshine making a daisy-chain. Can you count how many daisies she has joined together so far?

Blind Man's Buff

Toby is blindfolded – it is his job to find the other four children in the garden. They are making it hard for him – you, too! Look carefully to see where Lucy, Anna, David and Tom have hidden themselves.

HOW THE FOX CHEATED THE BEARCUBS

Beyond the glassy mountains and beyond silken meadows stood a dark forest. No one ever went there and no one had ever even seen it. In this forest in the very darkest undergrowth, lived a mother bear and her two cubs. When the cubs grew up, they decided they would go out into the world. So they made ready, said goodbye to mother bear and set off. They tramped and tramped for one whole day, then another, and finally they emerged from the forest into a meadow, and there they ate everything mother bear had given them for the journey. Not a crumb remained.

'Oh, little brother, I'm so hungry,' grumbled the younger bear cub.

'Just imagine how I feel, then!' sighed the older one.

So they trudged on and, as luck would have it, they found a round of cheese on the pathway. They wanted to divide it, but couldn't decide how best to do it. They began to argue, and they argued and argued until a fox ran up to them.

'What are you young fellows arguing about?' he asked them.

'Well, we've got a round of cheese and we don't know how to divide it fairly,' said the bear cubs.

'That's easy. I'll divide it for you,' said the fox, smiling to himself. He took the cheese from them and broke it into two pieces.

'That's not fairly divided,' shouted the bear cubs. 'One half is bigger than the other.'

The fox examined the two halves carefully and said: 'You're quite right, this half is a bit bigger. But we'll soon put that right,' and he bit off a piece from the larger half.

'Now the other half is bigger,' shouted the cubs. So the fox bit off a piece from the other half. But then the first half was again the bigger piece, and so it went on from one to the other. The fox bit off pieces from each half, until he had eaten both pieces and there was nothing left at all.

'Brother, that was a nice way to divide it up for us,' grumbled the bear cubs. 'You've eaten all the cheese yourself.'

'Indeed, I divided it very fairly between you,' laughed the fox. 'Neither of you got a crumb more nor a crumb less than the other.' And so saying, he ran off.

THE GIANT'S SPELL

A miller's apprentice called Jack was given a day off to do with as he liked.

'I shall wander through the countryside,' he told his master.

'Be careful,' the miller warned.

After several hours' walking, Jack came to a lonely valley where bushes and rocks were as high as houses. He marvelled at their size until he caught sight of a fawn tethered outside a cave. It looked at him with large eyes as he stroked it and gave it some grass to eat.

Suddenly a giant came storming out of the cave.

Jack was going to run off, but the fawn looked at him so sadly that he felt he must stay. He drew out his sword and stood guard. The giant roared with laughter.

'Do you imagine that will protect you?' he shouted loudly.

Jack quaked with fear, but he stood his ground. 'What harm have I done you?' he called up to the giant.

'None, you miserable wretch!' the giant replied. 'But I don't like your face and so I will destroy you.' And without another word he swung his club high in the air and brought it down, while the fawn trembled.

Fortunately Jack was a nimble lad and easily dodged the blow. Round and round he pranced as the giant spun himself round and round after the boy, but without success. The club kept crashing down on to the ground with such force that the land cracked beneath the giant.

It wasn't long at all before the giant grew so tired and dizzy that he fell to the ground and hit his head on a rock.

Jack had defeated the clumsy giant. At this moment of victory the fawn changed into a beautiful princess. The bushes became courtiers and the rocks became fine buildings.

'The giant was an evil spirit who bewitched my father's kingdom,' she told Jack, 'and I am pledged to marry the man who breaks the spell.' There and then Jack kissed her, and after that they married and lived happily for ever in the King's palace.

Here We Come

Honk! Honk! Honk!
Lorry on the road,
Bringing sacks of lumpy coal –
What a heavy load!

Whee-eee-eee!
Jet planes in the sky!
Leaving snowy trails of smoke
Way up high.

Chuff! Chuff! Chuff! –
Engine on the line,
Taking us on holiday
To have a happy time!

The Dwarf and the Squirrel

Not all dwarfs live beneath the earth, in Dwarfland. There are some who live in the fields and woods. This is all very well in summer, but not so good in the winter, when it is cold and food is scarce. Fitziputzi was a woodland dwarf. He lived under the roots of a beech tree.

In the winter, Fitziputzi had a terrible time trying to find enough for his wife and his ten hungry children to eat. He was on the move from early morning until late at night, and often all he found were a few beech nuts and a lonely turnip or two. At last there came a day when he couldn't find even these odds and ends, and in despair he went into the forest to find his friend, Springy the squirrel, who was always cheerful and helpful.

Springy was sitting on the branch of a fir tree.

'Fitziputzi!' He squeaked when he saw the dwarf. 'What are you doing in my forest on such a cold day?'

'You squirrels are so lucky,' sighed the hungry dwarf. 'When winter comes all you have to do is curl up in a ball and sleep through the worst weather, but I have to hunt all over the place for food to feed my starving family. Today,' he wailed, 'I haven't been able to find so much as a crumb.'

'Don't you worry,' said Springy at once. 'Just watch me!' And he started jumping all over the place. From branch to branch and from tree to tree he jumped and darted, gathering nuts from all his different store cupboards. 'Catch!' he called, and threw one nut after the other into the dwarf's sack. Soon the sack was almost too heavy to carry.

'Thank you so much,' Fitziputzi cried.

'Don't mention it,' smiled Springy.

It was just like Christmas to Fitziputzi as he marched through the snow.

Animal Forfeits

You will need a dice and a counter for each player. Throw a six in order to start, then move the number shown at each throw of the dice. The board has many forfeits. If anyone manages to get to home without performing a single forfeit, they will be the outright winner. Otherwise score ten points against each player for each forfeit they perform and the person with the lowest score wins.

The Two Gifts of Charity

In a certain village there once lived two women. They were neighbours. One was rich and miserly and the other would have shared all she had, but she was quite miserably poor.

One day an old beggar came to the village and begged the rich woman for a chunk of bread. But she turned him away, shouting angrily:

'Keep to your own people, I've nothing to give!"

So the beggar went to the poor woman. She invited him into her cottage and gave him a chunk of bread she was just preparing for her children's dinner.

'What I have, I give,' she said. 'There's not much, but I've nothing more.'

The beggar thanked her kindly and, as he left he said:

'God bless you, and whatever you start now, go on doing until sundown!'

Then the beggar departed and the poor woman began to wonder what she should give the children to eat. There was not a potato in the cottage and she had given the last piece of bread to the beggar. She had only a few lengths of linen material from which she had intended to make shirts for the children. But one must eat, and so she decided to sell the linen and buy food with the money.

She picked up the linen and began measuring it. She measured and measured, and there was always some more linen. She went on measuring until sundown and counted several thousands of lengths. Then she remembered the beggar's words and realised how he had rewarded her.

The poor woman took the linen, sold it at the Spring Fair, bought two cows, a strip of land and a meadow, and still there was some money left over. So she lived contentedly with her children.

Her rich neighbour heard about it and was sorry that she had turned the beggar away.

A year passed, and one fine day the beggar appeared again in the village. The rich woman saw him, immediately invited him in and treated him to the best she had in the house. The beggar ate his fill, thanked her and, as he left, remarked:

'God bless you, and whatever you start now, go on doing till sundown!'

The woman already had some linen prepared and had decided that she would immediately begin measuring. But, at that moment, a chicken ran into the room and the woman started to chase it out. She chased it and chased it but the chicken always escaped her. She chased it all afternoon. And just as she chased it out of the house, the sun set!

CAN YOU BELIEVE YOUR EYES?

Daisies

These two daisies look very different. Can you guess which flower centre is the larger – a or b?

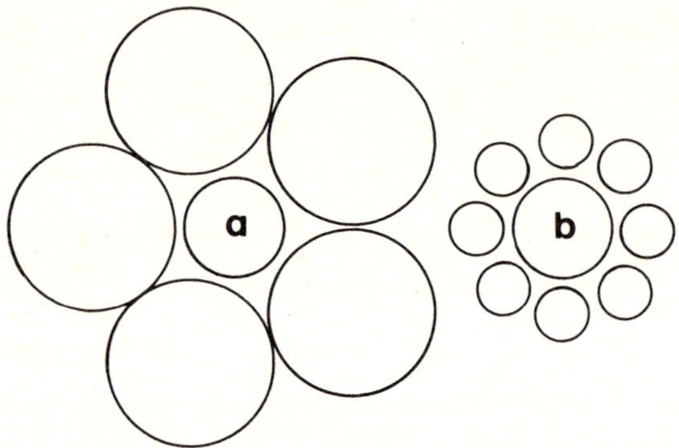

MYSTERY DOTS

Stare at the black squares for a while and soon you will see black dots appearing at the corners. Look at one mystery dot in particular and you'll find that it will disappear!

LINE UP

Can you guess which line joins up with a – is it b or c? You can check by using a ruler.

a

b c

SIZES

These buildings all vary in size. Can you put them in the correct order, from smallest to largest?

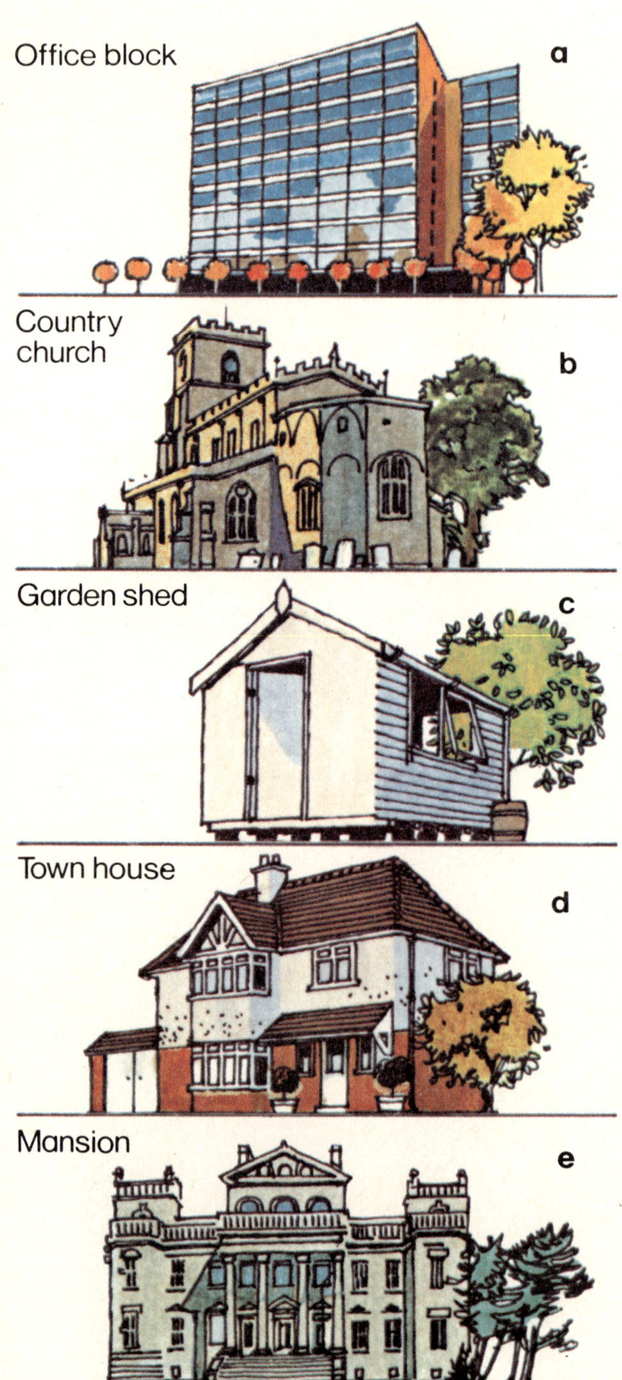

The Merchant and his Donkey

There was once a poor but hard-working merchant, and his little son, Abad. Once a week they went to market. The merchant rode the donkey, while his son, Abad, ran behind holding onto the donkey's tail.

One day some women saw them. 'Just look!' they cried. 'A cruel father lets his little son run behind. What a monster he must be to permit such a thing . . .'

Now, the merchant was a kind-hearted man, and when he heard this he jumped down. 'You ride, my son,' he said. 'I will walk behind.' But they had only gone a little way before they met another group who threw up their hands in horror at the sight of the old man walking.

'Lazy little rascal!' they all shouted, 'to let your father trail behind you in the dust!'

When he heard this, the merchant mounted his donkey behind his son, and was almost immediately soundly scolded for overloading his old donkey. Distressed and confused, the merchant said wearily, 'I know, we shall both walk behind.'

'Look! What madness!' shouted three old men as they saw this. And at the sound of their laughter, the merchant said sadly – 'Now I know it is impossible to please everyone!'

A DAY AT THE FAIR

Everyone loves to go to the fair! This fairground is packed with people enjoying themselves. What would you like to do – take a ride on the waltzer or on a carousel horse? Try the ghost train ride or try your luck on one of the side stalls? There's plenty to do and plenty to look at – and if you look carefully enough you will find ten deliberate mistakes.

THE POWER OF FRIENDSHIP

Once upon a time there were three friends: a stag, a tortoise and a bird. One night the stag got caught in a net set by a hunter. At first he tried to get free by his own efforts, but he soon realised that neither his antlers nor his hoofs could tear a hole in the net and he called to his friend, the tortoise, for help.

The tortoise came up and immediately began to gnaw through the strands one by one. But while the tortoise toiled away, the day began to dawn. The hunter who had set the trap got up, took his bows and arrows and set out for the forest.

Hardly had he entered the forest, when he was observed by the stag's other friend, the bird. To distract the hunter, the bird began flying above his head as though it were wounded. The hunter went after it, while the tortoise freed the stag.

When the hunter finally reached the net he found it gnawed through and empty. In his anger he seized his bow, took up his arrow and aimed at the bird. As he was about to shoot, the tortoise bit his toe. The hunter cried out, missing his target, and the bird flew away. The hunter then seized the tortoise, thrust it into his pouch and set off homeward. On the way he grew hungry. Sitting down in the shade of a tree, he started to eat his meal of rice cakes. As he sat there, the stag approached him from behind, gently lifted the pouch onto his antlers and sped away into the forest. There the bird was waiting for him.

It pierced the pouch with his beak and went on pecking at it until it had freed the tortoise.

Mimi and Pozo

Mimi and Pozo lived next door to each other, with only an old wooden fence to separate them. Mimi was a white cat and Pozo was a dachshund.

Although they both loved peace and quiet they grew very noisy when they caught sight of each other in their gardens. Pozo howled and barked, while Mimi arched her back and spat angrily.

Mimi's mistress and Pozo's master were so worried about it all.

'Those two animals would eat each other if there wasn't a fence between them,' one said to the other. 'All our neighbours are complaining about the noise.'

But what was to be done? Both the cat and the dog had to be let out for fresh air and exercise.

They did not notice that the boards of the old fence were rotten and so, one day, part of it fell down. At last Mimi and Pozo could face each other.

Full of rage they glared at each other. But what was this? Mimi saw that Pozo had a dear, funny face. Pozo saw that Mimi was soft and sweet. Suddenly they found they liked each other! And so ended their noisy battles and they were the best of friends from that day on.

The Talking Bottle

Once upon a time there was a bottle. He stood on the shelf for a long time with all his other brother bottles. But they all stood sadly, silently, because whenever one of them tried to talk, all that came out was a little 'hic'.

Then, one day, the bottle was taken off the shelf, carried in a paper bag, emptied, then thrown into the sea.

The sea was so rough and so big! But the bottle bobbed up and down and so he soon got used to it. No matter how often he was buried in the waves, he always bobbed up again!

And all the time the sea sang.

And the fishes came to look at him.

And a shark almost took a bite at him.

And all the while the sea sang her lovely song.

Sometimes she roared it very loudly, keeping company with the angry storm.

Sometimes she sang it sweet and low, serenading the moon.

But all the while she sang, the bottle listened until he had learned it all.

And then, finally, the bottle came gently to rest on a sandy beach, where he lay warming himself in the sun. A little boy picked him up and took him home.

And whenever the little boy wanted to listen, the talking bottle would sing to him his endless song of the sea.

The Artists

Three artists are busily painting the scene before them. They have been working away at their easels nearly all day, and now they have just added the finishing touches. All three pictures are very pretty, but only one of the artists has painted the scene accurately in every detail. Can you decide which picture this is?

Noah's Ark

The animals went in two by two – and here they all come – but look at each pair carefully to find three pairs that do not match correctly.

A Question of Honesty

Once upon a time a poor man stole an old broken pipe. As he was caught in the act, he was thrown into prison. In prison the thief was forgotton and he was kept there for many months without a trial, and he began to wonder how he could get out of prison. He couldn't escape, for there were too many guards and they watched him well. There was nothing for it but to be artful. One day he asked the guard to take him to see the king.

'Why do you want to see the king?' asked the guard.

'I want to give him a rare treasure,' answered the thief. And so they led him to the king.

'What do you want of me?' said the king when the thief stood before him.

'Your majesty, I want to present you with a rare treasure,' replied the thief, and he pulled out a piece of paper from his pocket.

'But that's just an ordinary pear pip,' exclaimed the king, when the thief had unwrapped the paper.

'Yes, it is a pear pip,' answered the thief, 'but a special sort of pear! If you plant it, it will grow into a tree, and golden pears will ripen on that tree!'

'Then, why don't you plant it yourself?' asked the king.

'There's a good reason,' said the thief. 'If the tree is to bear golden pears, it must be planted by a person who has never stolen and never cheated anyone. Otherwise it will bear only ordinary pears. And that is why I have brought

the pip to you, Your Majesty, because you surely have never stolen and never cheated anyone!'

'Oh, no, no, I can't do that!' said the king guardedly – because long ago, as a little boy, he had stolen some of his mother's golden coins.

'Well then, let your chancellor sow it,' said the thief.

'Oh, no, no, that's impossible,' said the chancellor guardedly – because he was prepared to accept bribes.

'Well, let the commander of the royal army sow it then,' proposed the thief.

'Oh, no, no, that's out of the question,' said the commander of the royal army, making some excuse, for he had often done the soldiers out of their pay.

'Well, the supreme judge then,' suggested the thief to the king.

But not even the supreme judge would hear a word of it, because he judged according to what people were prepared to pay.

'Then the warden of the prison,' advised the thief.

But the warden of the prison also refused to do it, because he accepted money from the prisoners and matched the severity of his treatment accordingly.

And so it went on and on. Whoever the thief suggested, seemed to have no desire to try to plant the tree with the golden pears. Each made some excuse, because he had something or other on his conscience. And, at last the thief began to laugh and said: 'The lot of you, whoever you are, all steal, cheat and lie, but you don't have to go to prison for it. And I, simply because I took an old broken pipe, have to stay there!' And when the king heard this and considered the matter, he decided to let the thief go.

THE LAND OF JUMPING JACKS

Long ago in the land of Jumping Jacks, there lived a king called King Cabbage.

King Cabbage was a horrible king and all his people were afraid of him. No one was allowed to walk or skip or run. Everyone had to jump. King Cabbage made his soldiers jump in the palace, the fathers had to jump to work and the children had to jump all the way to school.

All this jumping in the land of Jumping Jacks made the soldiers and the fathers and the children so tired that they cried. But nasty King Cabbage would laugh at them and shout: 'You must jump so high you touch the sky. Come on – jump, jump, jump!'

One day, King Cabbage was riding his horse in the forest and making all his soldiers jump to keep up with him, when suddenly a little old lady dressed in a green cloak appeared in front of him – and she was walking! The king was very angry indeed and amazed to see someone disobeying his orders. The soldiers were dumbfounded.

'Stop!' shouted the king. 'This is the land of Jumping Jacks. Running, skipping or walking is not allowed. I am the king and I command you to jump or I will have you thrown into the palace dungeons!'

The little old lady took no notice and went on walking.

King Cabbage turned purple with rage. But the old lady did not seem at all frightened, although the king's soldiers were quaking with fear.

'Seize her immediately,' the king screamed at his soldiers.

The soldiers started to jump toward the old lady and then stopped as she turned slowly to face the king. Then, from under her cloak she drew a handful of magic seeds and threw them over King Cabbage.

She glared at him as she muttered a spell. 'From this day forward may your skin match the evil of your heart, and may you jump for ever after!'

In a flash King Cabbage was changed into an ugly toad, and with horrible croaking sounds he jumped away into the forest, never to be seen again. And thereafter his kingdom ceased to be the land of the Jumping Jacks since everyone was quite free to walk around happily and at their leisure!

The race is on – the boats are skimming down the river and the crews of eight oarsmen are working hard. Look carefully at the scene and find the deliberate mistake.

Here are five pretty girls all dressed in the national costume of their country. Can you match each girl with her country?

Russia
Spain
Scotland
Holland
Japan

Curly Tails

The mother pig is in her sty at feeding time. Her little piglets are busy feeding and all we can see are their curly tails. Only two piglets have the same curl in their tails. Can you find them?

Never-Never-Land

Now I will tell you about a country that everyone would like to visit, but no one knows how to reach. The road to it is long and arduous, uphill most of the way, and the only people who ever get there are those who are hot in the winter or cold in the summer. The country is called Never-Never-Land, where the roofs of the houses are made of pancakes, the doors and walls of marzipan, the beams of salami. Around each house there is a fence made of liver sausage and chippolatas. There are pumps and fountains that run with beer, wine and lemonade, which spurt into your mouth just for the asking. The streams run with milk, and the willows on the banks are hung with fresh rolls and buns.

In this Never-Never-Land the fish in the rivers are already fried or grilled, boiled or salted. If you are lazy, you only have to lie down on the bank and say 'Pst, Pst,' and a fish will jump out of the water into your lap.

And believe it or not, the birds that fly through the air are also nicely cooked. There are roast geese and roast ducks, roast pigeons and chickens, which fly quite happily straight into your mouth. You may trip over large stones and pebbles made of cheese and meat pastes and stuffings. When it rains it simply rains drops of honey. The snow is made of powdered sugar, the hail stones are sugar candy and almonds.

In this Never-Never-Land there are also large forests and instead of leaves the trees grow jackets and shirts and trousers in all colours. You also find the flowering shrubs decked with gorgeous dresses made of silk and satin, velvet and taffeta. You just pick whichever clothes take your fancy. Watches grow on the pine trees, shoes on the fir trees, and rings and necklaces on the larch trees.

If anyone is old or sick he just goes to the public baths. There he becomes young again and as healthy and as lively as a cricket. For every hour a person lazes away, he is paid a gold sovereign, and for snoring there's an extra gold sovereign as a bonus. Money can be found growing on trees.

But the real problem is that this country is surrounded by a great rampart of tapioca pudding and whoever wants to get to Never-Never-Land must eat his way through every mouthful. You'll have to wait until you have a huge appetite, before you can attempt to reach this magic Never-Never-Land!

The Ant and the Tapir

An ant once met a tapir by a river running through the forest:

'Where are you off to, little fellow?'

'What do you mean little fellow?' said the ant. 'I am the strongest creature in the forest.'

'Oh, no, I am the strongest creature in the forest!' said the tapir.

'Very well! Come here tomorrow at the same time and we'll wrestle. Then we'll see who is the stronger.'

'How can I wrestle with you? I can hardly see you.'

'We'll have a tug-o'-war.'

Then the ant went to the river and said to the crocodile:

'I have prepared a feast for you, crocodile. Come to the bank of the river at this time tomorrow morning and there will be a goose here, tied to a rope.'

'That's very good of you, ant,' said the crocodile. 'Thank you very much.'

The next morning when the ant met the tapir he handed him the end of a rope.

'Tie this rope to your leg,' said the ant, 'and I'll tie my leg to the other end. When I say ready, then pull and we'll see who is the stronger.'

The tapir tied one end to his leg and the ant ran off with the other to the crocodile. The latter was already waiting for him a little way along the bank. The ant tied the other end of the rope to his tail and said:

'And now pull! But don't make a sound, so that the goose doesn't fly away.'

So the crocodile pulled and the tapir pulled.

'I would never have thought that an ant had such strength,' said the tapir to himself, and he pulled with all his might. But he couldn't budge an inch from the spot.

'It's incredible that I can't pull a goose into the river,' thought the crocodile to himself, and he also tugged with all his might, but in vain.

And so they tugged and pulled. And just then some people came sailing down the river in a boat, and they laughed to see the tapir and the crocodile tugging away at each other.

So they cut the rope and nobody won the tug-o'-war!

Wishes

These are the things
Which I'd like best;
To find the bluebird
In its nest,
To catch the coloured sparks
That fly
From a rocket
In the sky.
To have a camel
Of my own,
And ride the desert
All alone.
Which are the things
You'd like to do?
You tell me,
Now I've told you.

Answers

Page 11
Three Skiers: The skier in picture 1 is different. Right eye; Single stripe on back of skis; Base of ski pole; Stripes on hat; Fold in jacket missing, to the right of zip; Extra length of zip on anorak.
Odd One Out: The frog (d) cannot fly.

Page 14
Sparrows' Supper: 4 grains each.

Page 16
Catch the Runaway Bull: Farmhand (b) has caught the bull.
Matching Toys: 1-b; 2-a; 3-d; 4-c; 5-e.

Page 20
Mixed-Up Masks: a-5; b-6; c-1; d-2; e-3; f-4.
Pirate's Puzzle: The sides of the square are straight.

Page 25
The Entertainers: a-5; b-3; c-4; d-1; e-2.

Page 26
Hunt for the Fox: Under the feet of the third dog from the left.

Page 28
The Invisible Visitors: 6 snakes are hidden in the trees.
Mothers' Mix-Up: a-2; b-3; c-1; d-5; e-4.

Page 34
Tea Time: 15 dishes

Page 38
What Do You See?: Two fish or one octopus.
Tiger Twins: Rajah and Samson are tigers a and d.
Fancy Dress Party: The bunny is the only animal fancy dress costume.

Page 41
Musical Mix-Up: a-3; b-4; c-2; d-1; e-5; f-6.
The Clockwork Train: 18 passengers.

Page 47
Midsummer Day: Girl 1 has lost her ribbon.
Valiant Adventurers: a-4; b-1; c-2; d-3.

Page 50
Double Take: Two old men.
Match the Mermaids: a-4; b-3; c-2; d does not match 1.
Carousel Cavalcade: a and e are alike.

Page 53
Firework Night: 12 blue stars, 13 white stars, 5 sparklers, 14 people.

Page 56
Things We Need: Sheep – Winter clothes (a-5); Tree – Chair (b-1); Cow – Milk (c-4); Bee – Honey (d-2); Wheatsheaf – Bread (e-3); Chicken – Egg (f-6).

Page 58
Witches: 4 lanterns. **The Orchard:** 240 trees. **A Musical Family:** flute. **The Oyster Catcher:** 77 oysters.

Page 62
Picnic Packing: Cake, spoon, bottle, two bananas, a flask, two tomatoes, bread, mug, knife, orange, biscuits, glass.

Indian Signals: Hide!
Easter Parade: b (red flower becomes a red butterfly).

Page 67
Four Seasons: a – spring; b – summer; c – autumn; d – winter.
Deliberate mistakes: (a) Extra window in house; (b) Single track path; (c) Extra tree; (d) One tree missing.
Snowflake Patterns: (a) odd one is 1; (b) odd one is 3; (c) odd one is 3.

Page 70
The Football Team: Fourth boy from left has shirt on back to front.
Daisy-chain: Kitty has joined 22 daisies in a chain.

Page 78
Can You Believe Your Eyes?
Daisies: The two flower centres a and b are exactly the same size.
Line up: Line b joins up with line a.
Sizes: (c) Garden shed; (d) Town House; (b) Country church; (e) Mansion; (a) Office block.

Page 80
A Day at the Fair: (1) Chains missing from one chair on swing; (2) Men throwing coconuts at the shy; (3) Man wearing one shoe, one wellington boot; (4) Man with tie round wrong way; (5) Girl holding stick, balloon missing; (6) Girl holding mouse in bag instead of goldfish; (7) Roundabout, one horse going backwards; (8) Top of helter skelter slide wrong way round; (9) People and chairs all upside down on big wheel; (10) Girl on chair swing, travelling wrong way.

Page 83
The Artists: Picture a is the only accurate painting.
Noah's Ark: The wrong pairs – zebra and horse, hippo and rhino, reindeer and moose.

Page 87
The Boat Race: Left-hand boat has seven oarsmen.
National Costumes: Holland – a; Scotland – c; Spain – b; Japan – e; Russia – d.
Curly Tails: 5 and 8 are alike.